Compassion: The Only Way to Peace

An Address by Her Holiness
Sri Mata Amritanandamayi Devi

delivered at
Cinéma Vérité's 2007 Film Festival

12 October 2007 – Paris, France

Translated by
Swami Amritaswarupananda Puri

Compassion: The Only Way to Peace

Translated by Swami Amritaswarupananda Puri

Published by
  Mata Amritanandamayi Mission Trust
  Amritapuri P.O., Kollam Dt.,
  Kerala 690 525, India
  E-mail: info@theammashop.org

  Website: www.amritapuri.org
  Phone: (0476) 2896278, 2897578, 2896179, 2896399

Copyright © 2008 by Mata Amritanandamayi Mission Trust

All rights reserved. No part of this publication may be stored in a retrieval system, transmitted, reproduced, transcribed or translated into any language, in any form, by any means without the prior agreement and written permission of the publisher.

First Edition: May 2008
Second printing: June 2009
Third printing: June 2010
Fourth printing: June 2012
Fifth printing: June 2013

Introduction

In October 2007, the French film association Cinéma Vérité requested Amma to deliver an address on the increasing incidents of manmade and natural disasters in the world today. Cinéma Vérité had become aware of Amma as a unique spiritual leader and humanitarian through Jan Kounen's 2005 documentary *Darshan: The Embrace*. The organization has long focused on creating awareness regarding human-rights issues through film. Inspired by Kounen's depiction of Amma, Cinéma Vérité felt the time was right to begin presenting an annual Cinéma Vérité Award to individuals engaged in extraordinary work towards establishing world peace and harmony. Amma would be their first honouree.

The function took place in the centre of Paris in an art theatre at Place de la Bastille as part

Introduction

of Cinéma Vérité's 2007 Film Festival. Other dignitaries participating in the festival were the 1997 Nobel Laureate for Peace Jody Williams, Academy Award-nominated actress Sharon Stone and social and human-rights advocate Bianca Jagger.

Amma was introduced and welcomed by both Ms. Stone and Kounen. "There verily is no one more qualified to speak about peace than Amma," said Kounen. "Not only is her life *lived* in peace, it *awakens* peace. ... We are delighted to have this opportunity to honour Amma with the first annual Cinéma Vérité Award for her contribution towards world peace and harmony."

Kounen then went on to speak about his experience filming Amma, referring to her as a human with the power to transform others. "I am fortunate to be a director who can choose the topics of his films," he said. "This gave me the chance to spend time with Amma and have the opportunity to discover what she does and to come to understand the reality of who she is. This allowed me to go on a journey, and to bring something back from that journey—this film. It has provided me the chance to communicate to others who Amma is—what could be seen, perceived, experienced during the time I spent with Amma. This allowed me both the opportunity to pass on the message to others and to witness a human being who can transform others."

Kounen, who has directed both feature films and a number of documentaries on mystical cultures, said that his experience filming Amma was unique. "I personally have treated matters relating to spirituality, to healers, to miracle-makers. But with Amma, I found that the magic is something you can actually see, something she is doing right before your eyes. That is the most striking thing about her. Things you can see with your own eyes. And you simply have to capture it on film—to see it and give others an opportunity to also see. I would like to thank her for having given me the opportunity to make this film. Thank you."

Sharon Stone was the next to speak about Amma. "To introduce a saint is a big job," she said. "To film an angel is something else entirely. The film *Darshan* is extraordinarily inspiring. But the life of a person who gives himself in service

Academy Award-nominated actress Sharon Stone presented Amma with the the first annual Cinéma Vérité Award for her contribution towards world peace and harmony.

Compassion: The Only Way to Peace

is something that we can all aspire to. Because it is a choice. It is a choice to lend yourself to the service of others. As Milton said when he was losing his sight, 'Simply to stand and wait can be of service, to stand and wait on another.' We are in a time in the world when it is more a time of need than any other. We are in a time when we must stand and wait before we decide our action. Because we must do the thing of goodness. We must do the thing of kindness. And we must do the thing of grace.

"Amma has done the thing of grace with her entire life. She has embraced 26 million people. But she has done this as an action not only of giving, but as an action of example—an example of giving, and of goodness, of thoughtfulness and of waiting on others. Of waiting on them to take her embrace and to apply it to a life of goodness. Please welcome not only this saint and this angel but this person of active goodness."

As a token of Cinéma Vérité's appreciation of Amma and her work, Ms. Stone then presented Amma with a silver necklace and locket, which

Introduction

brought forth a loud round of applause from the theatre.

In her address, "Compassion: The Only Way to Peace," Amma offered a realistic and constructive analysis of the problems facing the world today, pointing to specific areas of disharmony and how only a compassionate outlook can bring about their rectification.

With regards to conflict, Amma was extremely frank. "Since the beginning of the world, there has been conflict," she said. "Saying that it's impossible to totally eradicate it causes a lot of anxiety. But it's the truth, isn't it?"

While accepting that conflict cannot be totally eradicated, Amma lamented the deterioration of war in terms of ethics and code of conduct. She explained how in olden times foot soldiers only fought with foot soldiers, horsemen with horsemen, etc.; how one was not allowed to attack an unarmed soldier or to hurt women or children; how fighting would stop at sunset and resume only at sunrise. "Such was the great tradition of *dharmic* wars, in which the enemy was considered with respect and kindness, both on and off the battlefield. The sentiments and the culture of the citizens of the enemy kingdom were also respected. Such was the courageous outlook of the people living then."

Amma said that modern warfare was something completely different: "In wars today, the enemy's country is destroyed in every possible way. Conquerors plunder and monopolize the land, natural resources and wealth of the defeated country and use them for their own selfish enjoyment. The culture and traditions that have been passed down for generations are uprooted, and innocent people are killed without mercy."

Amma said that because of the violence and suffering mankind has brought about due to greed and hatred, humanity has taken upon itself "countless curses." "In order to attain freedom from these curses, at least a hundred generations to come should wipe the tears of the suffering, striving to console them and alleviate their pain," Amma said. "At least now, as an atonement, shouldn't we try to introspect?"

Introduction

Furthermore, Amma requested world-leaders to abandon their old notions and ideas regarding war. "It is time to end the cruelty and ruthlessness man has shown in the name of war," she said. "War is the product of uncivilised minds. These thought patterns need to fall away and be replaced by the new leaves, blossoms and fruit of compassion and beauty. Gradually, we can destroy the inner demon—the "desire for war"—which is a curse upon both humanity and Nature. We can then enter a new era of peace and happiness."

The next area of conflict Amma addressed was that between science and religion. "Religion and science should go hand in hand," Amma said. "Both science without religion and religion without science are incomplete. But society is trying to segregate us into religious people and scientific people." Amma asserted that in truth science and religion are quite similar in their pursuits—one being an investigation in the external laboratory, the other in the internal. Amma said: "'What is the nature of the experienced world?' 'How does it function in perfect harmony?' 'From where did it come?' 'Where is it going?' 'Where will it lead?' 'Who am I?' ... Who asks these kinds of questions—people of faith or people of science? Both do."

"We should learn lessons from history, but we shouldn't live there," Amma concluded. "The fusion of science and spirituality will help us come out of the dark corridors of the past and into the light of peace, harmony and unity."

Amma also spoke about inter-religious conflict, saying that due to mankind's narrow-mindedness and ignorance, movements that were intended as sources of light instead cast shadows. "Spirituality is the key with which we can open our hearts and see everyone with compassion," Amma said. "But being blinded by selfishness, our minds have lost their proper judgment and our vision has become distorted. This selfishness only creates more darkness. Using the very same key with which we could open our hearts, our indiscriminate mindset locks them shut instead."

A large part of Amma's speech focused on the increasing disharmony between man and Nature, and its dire repercussions—earthquakes, tsunamis, global warming, extreme weather, droughts, etc.

Introduction

Again, Amma compared the current situation to that of days gone by. "In the old days, there was no specific need for environmental preservation because protecting Nature was part of worshiping God and life itself," Amma said. "More than remembering 'God,' the people used to love and serve Nature and society. They saw the Creator through the creation. They loved, worshiped and protected Nature as the visible form of God. Let us try to reawaken this attitude. At present, the biggest threat to mankind is not a third world war, but the loss of Nature's harmony and our widening separation from Nature. We should develop the awareness of a person at gunpoint. Only then can humanity survive."

Amma gave a number of suggestions on how to restore the lost harmony between mankind and Nature: increased pollutant restrictions on factories, car-pooling and travelling short distances by foot or bicycle, the maintaining of family vegetable gardens, and the planting of at least one tree a month by every individual.

"Nature is our first mother," Amma said. "She nurtures us throughout our lives. Our birth mother may allow us to sit on her lap for a couple of years, but Mother Nature patiently bears our weight our entire life. She sings us to sleep, feeds us and caresses us. Just as a child is obligated to his birth mother, we should all feel an obligation and responsibility towards Mother Nature. If we forget this responsibility, it is equal to forgetting our own self. If we forget Nature, we will cease to exist, for to do so is to walk towards death."

Throughout her speech, Amma continually stressed the conviction that, with regard to all these areas of conflict, compassion is the only true solution. "Compassion is the foundation of peace," Amma said. "Compassion resides within everyone. But it is difficult to experience it and express it in all of our actions. We must turn inwards to search deep within ourselves. ... If we want to bring peace to the external world, first our inner world needs to be at peace."

Simultaneously translated via headset into both English and French, Amma's address was met with a thunderous round of applause. Thereafter, the night concluded not in words, but in

Introduction

action—Amma lovingly embracing each one of the program's attendees with her heartfelt *darshan*.

Swami Amritaswarupananda Puri
Vice-Chairman
Mata Amritanandamayi Math

Compassion:
The Only Way to Peace

By Her Holiness Sri Mata Amritanandamayi Devi

12 October 2007 – Paris, France

Since the beginning of the world, there has been conflict. Saying that it's impossible to totally eradicate it causes a lot of anxiety. But it's the truth, isn't it? The reason being that good and evil will always exist in the world. In our struggle to accept the good and reject the bad, the possibility of conflict cannot be completely ruled out. Such conflict has manifested in nearly all countries in forms such as internal strife, war and strikes. Although most wars are generally aimed at protecting vested interests, there have been rare circumstances where the needs of the people were taken into consideration and a greater good was achieved.

Compassion: The Only Way to Peace

Unfortunately, the majority of wars waged by man have not been fought to uphold truth and justice but have been motivated by selfishness.

From approximately 5,000 years ago until the rule of the great Indian king Chandragupta Maurya, founder of the Maurya Dynasty, truth and *dharma* [righteousness] played a central role in all wars fought in India. Even back then, defeating and, if need be, destroying the enemy was a part of war. However, there were clear rules that had to be followed on the battlefield and during combat.

For example, foot soldiers were only allowed to fight with foot soldiers and horsemen could only fight with horsemen. Warriors riding elephants or in chariots could only fight with similarly mounted opponents. The same rules applied to those fighting with maces, swords, spears and bow-and-arrows. A soldier was not allowed to attack injured or unarmed soldiers, nor would he harm women, children, the elderly or the sick. Battles began at dawn with the blowing of a conch and ended exactly at sunset, with the soldiers of both sides forgetting their mutual enmity and dining together as one. Battle would then resume the next morning at sunrise.

There were even incidents of victorious kings happily returning the entire kingdom and all the riches they had won to the king they had defeated, or his rightful heir. Such was the great tradition of dharmic wars, in which the enemy was considered with respect and kindness, both on and off the battlefield. The sentiments and the culture of the citizens of the enemy kingdom were also respected. Such was the courageous outlook of the people living then.

These days, to prevent terrorist attacks, strict security measures are implemented in airports and other establishments. While such measures are necessary for our physical safety, they are not a final solution. In fact, there is one explosive in particular that is the most destructive of all. No machine can detect it. It is the hatred, loathing and vengeance found in the human mind.

In this regard, Amma remembers a story.

The head of a certain village was celebrating his 100th birthday. Many dignitaries and news reporters attended his party. One of the reporters asked him, "What are you most proud of in this long life of yours?"

The old man answered, "Well, I've lived 100 years, and I don't have a single enemy on this planet."

"Really? Isn't that amazing!" the reporter remarked. "May your life be an inspiration to all! Now, tell me, how is this possible?"

"Well," the old man replied, "It is very simple. I made sure that none of them remained alive!"

If we don't eradicate our destructive emotions, there will be no end to war and violence.

In wars today, the enemy's country is destroyed in every possible way. Conquerors plunder and monopolize the land, natural resources and wealth of the defeated country and use them for their own selfish enjoyment. The culture and traditions that have been passed down for generations are uprooted, and innocent people are killed without mercy.

Furthermore, we cannot begin to fathom the amount of toxic fumes emitted by bombs and other weapons of war, filling the atmosphere and polluting the soil. How many generations are forced to suffer physically and mentally as a consequence! In the wake of war, all that is left are death, poverty, starvation and epidemics. Such are war's gifts to humanity.

Today, some wealthy countries instigate wars simply to promote the sale of their latest weapons. No matter what action we perform, even if it be war, the goal should be the protection of truth and dharma. Amma's not saying that war is unavoidable. In principle, there is never a time when war is necessary. But will we ever be able to completely eradicate war from the external world as long as conflict remains in the minds of man? This is something we really should contemplate.

One of the main reasons for many conflicts in today's world is the separation between science and religion. Actually, religion and science should go hand in hand. Both science without religion and religion without science are incomplete.

But society is trying to segregate us into religious people and scientific people. Scientists claim religion and spirituality are based on blind faith, whereas science is fact because it has been proven through experimentation. Their question is: Which side are you on? Faith or proven fact?

It is inaccurate to say religion and spirituality are based on blind faith and that their principles have not been proven. In fact, spiritual masters may have undertaken even more exhaustive research than modern scientists. Just as modern scientists research the external world, the great sages conducted research in the inner laboratories of their minds. From this point of view, they too were scientists. In reality, the foundation of true religion is not blind faith; it is *sraddha*. Sraddha is enquiry—an intense exploration within one's own self.

What is the nature of the experienced world? How does it function in perfect harmony? From where did it come? Where is it going? Where will it lead? Who am I? Such was their enquiry. Who asks these kinds of questions—people of faith or people of science? Both do.

The sages of the past were not only great intellectuals; they were seers who had realized the Truth. Intellectuals are definitely an asset to society. However, mere words and thoughts are not enough. It is the people who live those principles who actually breathe life and beauty into those words and thoughts.

Long ago, there was a *mahatma* [great soul], who wrote a book titled *Compassion in Life*. To raise funds to publish the book, he invited people he knew to sponsor it. However, just as he was about to send the book to the press, a famine broke out in his village and many people began dying. Without a second thought, he used the money meant for printing the book to feed the poor and hungry. The sponsors were upset. They asked, "What have you done? How will we print the book? Poverty and starvation are common occurrences. Birth and death are always taking place in this world. It was not right to spend so much money in the name of this natural calamity." The mahatma didn't reply, but only smiled in return.

After some time, he returned to the benefactors with the request of printing the book. Though they were hesitant, they agreed. But the day before the book was to go to print, there was a huge flood. Thousands died and many more lost their homes and possessions. Again, the mahatma used all the money to help the disaster victims. This time, the sponsors were even more upset. They spoke harshly to him. But as before, he did not react to their words and only smiled in return.

When the book was finally printed, it was titled *Compassion in Life: Volume Three*. Enraged, the sponsors demanded, "Hey, aren't you supposed to be a *sannyasi*—a follower of truth? How can you lie like this? How can this book be the 'third' volume? Where are the first and second volumes? Are you trying to make fools of us?"

The mahatma answered, "Actually, this is the book's third volume. The first volume was when the village was suffering from the famine. The second volume was when thousands of innocent people's lives and possessions were washed away by the flood. The first two volumes showed us how to bring compassion into our lives at a practical level. My dear friends, books are only inert words. When a living human being cries out for help, if we are unable to lend a loving hand to help him, then what is the point of a book describing compassion?"

If we want to bring life and consciousness into our words and thoughts, we have to put them into action. To achieve this goal, we should search for a path in which religion and modern science move forward in harmony. This unity should not be a mere external show. We need to take resolute action to understand and integrate the aspects of religion and science that are beneficial to society.

If one's mind is purely scientific, it will not be compassionate. The tendency of such a mind will only be to attack, overpower and harass others. However, when a scientific intellect comes together with an understanding of spirituality—the inner essence of religion—compassion and sympathy for all living beings arise spontaneously.

World history is primarily comprised of stories fraught with hostility, revenge and hatred. The rivers of blood spilled by man in his attempt to seize everything for himself and bring everyone under his thumb have yet to run dry. In fact, when we look into the past, it may seem as though the human race has not possessed even an iota of compassion, so cruel have been our actions.

Compassion: The Only Way to Peace

We should learn lessons from history, but we should not live there. The fusion of science and spirituality will help us come out of the dark corridors of the past and into the light of peace, harmony and unity.

Spirituality is the key with which we can open our hearts and see everyone with compassion. But being blinded by selfishness, our minds have lost their proper judgment and our vision has become distorted. This selfishness only creates more darkness. Using the very same key with which we could open our hearts, our indiscriminate mindset locks them shut instead.

There is a story about four men who were on their way to attend a religious conference and had to spend the night together on an island. It was a bitter-cold night. Each traveller carried a small bundle of firewood and a matchbox in his pack, and each thought he was the only one with firewood and matches.

One of the men reasoned, "Judging from the medallion around that man's neck, I would say he is from some other religion. If I start a fire, he will also benefit from the warmth. Why should I use my precious wood to warm him?"

The second man thought, "That man is from the country that has always fought against us. I wouldn't dream of using my wood to make him comfortable!"

The third man looked at one of the others and justified, "I know that fellow. He belongs to a sect that is always creating problems in my religion. I'm not going to waste my wood for his sake!"

The fourth man brooded, "That man's skin is a different colour, and I hate that! There's no way I'm going to use my wood for him!"

In the end, not one of them was willing to light his wood to warm the others, and so, by morning, they all froze to death. Similarly, we harbour enmity towards others in the name of religion, nationality, colour and caste, without extending compassion towards our fellow beings.

In the name of peace, we hold a lot of conferences. But how much change can we really hope to bring about by simply sitting around a table, talking? When all is said and done and we shake hands in parting, is that gesture an actual expression of a warmth of love and compassion felt in our hearts? If not, a real dialogue has not taken place. For a real dialogue, there must be open and heartfelt oneness and the walls constructed by hostility, preconceived notions and vengeance must disappear.

Everyone is concerned about the issue of environmental protection. However, we fail to notice the lessons Nature is trying to teach us. Just observe Nature in winter. The trees shed their old leaves. They no longer bear fruit. Even birds rarely perch on trees then. But as spring arrives, all of Nature is transformed. New leaves sprout from the trees and vines, and soon the trees blossom with flowers and fruit. Birds flutter their wings, and their chirping can be heard everywhere. The whole environment itself becomes fragrant and permeated with vitality. The very same trees that, just a few months before, seemed to be withering away are now bursting with new life and beauty.

Taking this example from Nature, countries and their leaders should abandon their old notions and ideas regarding war. It is time to end the cruelty and ruthlessness man has shown in the name of war. War is the product of uncivilised minds. These thought patterns need to fall away and be replaced by the new leaves, blossoms and fruit of compassion and beauty. Gradually, we can destroy the inner demon—the "desire for war"—which is a curse upon both humanity and Nature. We can then enter a new era of peace and happiness.

Compassion is the foundation of peace. Compassion resides within everyone. But it is difficult to experience it and express it in all of our actions. We must turn inwards to search deep within ourselves. "Is my heart still vibrant with life? Can I still experience the source of love and compassion within me? Does my heart still melt at the pain and sorrow of others? Have I cried along with those who are suffering? Have I really tried to wipe another's tears to console them or given someone at least a single meal or a set of clothing?" Like this, we can honestly introspect. Then the soothing moonlight of compassion will spontaneously shine within our minds.

If we want to bring peace to the external world, first our inner world needs to be at peace. Peace is not an intellectual resolve. It is an experience.

Compassion: The Only Way to Peace

Compassion and congeniality make a leader truly courageous. Anyone who has wealth, weaponry and the know-how can wage a war. But no one can defeat the power of love and heartfelt oneness.

If only our minds, eyes, ears and hands could genuinely understand and feel the sorrow and pain of others! How many suicides could have been avoided? How many people could have received food, clothing and shelter? How many children could have been kept from becoming orphans? How many women who sell their bodies for a living could have been helped? How many sick people suffering from unbearable pain could have been provided medicine and treatment? How many conflicts in the name of money, fame and position could have been avoided?

The first step in developing compassion is to treat all objects we regard as inanimate—such as stones, sand, rocks and wood, etc.—with love and respect. If we can feel love and sympathy towards inanimate objects, it becomes easier to develop love and compassion towards trees, vines, birds, animals, the life in oceans, rivers, mountains and all the rest of Nature. If we can reach this state, then we will automatically have compassion towards all of mankind.

Shouldn't we give thanks to the chair and rocks, which provide us a place to sit and rest? Shouldn't we express our gratitude to Mother Earth, who patiently provides her lap for us to run, jump and play upon? Shouldn't we be grateful to the birds that sing for us, the flowers that blossom for us, the trees that provide us with shade and the rivers that flow for us?

Each dawn, we are greeted with a new sunrise. At night when we forget everything and sleep, anything could happen to us, even death. Do we ever thank the Great Power that blesses us to wake up the next morning and function just as before without anything having happened to our body or mind? If we look at it in this way, shouldn't we be grateful to everyone and everything? Only compassionate people are able to express gratitude.

There is no end to the war and death caused by man or to the tears shed by all the innocent victims of such tragedies. What were all these

Compassion: The Only Way to Peace

for? Only for conquering, establishing superiority and satisfying our greed for money and fame. Mankind has taken upon itself countless curses. In order to attain freedom from these curses, at least a hundred generations to come should wipe the tears of the suffering, striving to console them and alleviate their pain. At least now, as an atonement, shouldn't we try to introspect?

No power-hungry, self-centred leader bent on protecting his own interests has ever attained peace and happiness by conquering the world and persecuting people. Their deaths and the days leading up to them were hell on earth. History has proven this great truth. We should accept with gratitude this precious opportunity and move forward along the path of peace and compassion.

We neither bring anything nor take anything with us when we leave this world. We have to learn to be dispassionate and detached from the world and its objects, realizing that they will never give us everlasting, true happiness.

As you all know, Alexander the Great was a warrior and ruler who conquered nearly one-third of the world. He wanted to become the emperor of the entire world, but when defeated in battle, he fell sick with a terminal illness. A few days before his death, Alexander called his ministers to discuss his burial details. He described how he would like openings made on either side of his coffin, through which his arms should be kept hanging out, palms spread open. The ministers asked their lord why he wanted this to be done.

Alexander explained that, in this way, everyone would come to know that the "Great Alexander," who had dedicated his whole life to possessing and conquering, had left the world totally empty-handed. He had not even taken his own body with him. Therefore, they would understand how futile it is to spend one's life chasing after possessions.

We need to understand the impermanence of the world and its objects. They are temporary and can never come with us after death.

There is a rhythm to everything in the cosmos. The wind, the rain, the waves, the flow of our breath and our heartbeat—everything has a rhythm. Similarly, there is a rhythm in life. Our thoughts and actions create the rhythm and melody of our lives. When the rhythm of our thoughts is lost, it reflects in our actions. This will, in turn, throw off the very rhythm of life. Today, this is what we are seeing all around us.

Today, the air is becoming more and more polluted; the water as well. Rivers are drying up. Forests are being destroyed. New diseases are spreading. If this continues, a huge disaster is in store for all of Nature and humanity.

Amma will give an example to illustrate the effects of pollution on the environment. Amma still remembers how in her childhood, when a child got a scrape or small cut, its mother would cover the wound with cow dung. This would help it heal more rapidly. But if we were to do this today, the wound would become infected. One could even die. Today, cow dung is toxic. What was previously medicinal has today become poisonous.

The current generation lives as if it has no relationship with Nature. Everything around us is artificial. Today, we eat fruit and grains grown with artificial fertilizers and pesticides. We add preservatives to increase their shelf life. Like this, consciously or unconsciously, we are continuously eating poison. As a result, so many new diseases are appearing. In fact, long ago, the average lifespan was more than 100. But today people only live 80 years or less and more than 75 percent of the population suffer from some disease or other.

Not only has the food we eat and the water we drink become polluted, even the air we breathe has become full of toxins. Because of this, humanity's immune system is weakening. Already, so many people depend on inhalers to breathe, and this number is continually increasing. In a few years, we may have to walk around with air tanks to breathe, like astronauts in outer space. Most people today are allergic to something or other, even to the most seemingly insignificant things. Due to our increasing alienation from Nature, it is becoming more difficult for us to survive.

Today, not only people, but even the animals and plants we raise and cultivate are disconnecting from Nature. Wild plants survive regardless of the weather, adapting to Nature's conditions. But house plants cannot withstand pests on their own and have to be sprayed with pesticides. They need so much special care that they are unable to survive naturally.

Forests are being destroyed and apartment complexes erected in their place. Many birds build nests in these complexes. If we take a close look at these nests, we will see that they have been made with wires and pieces of plastic. This is because trees are decreasing. In the future, there may be no trees at all. The birds are learning to adapt to their new environment.

The condition of the honey bees is similar. Usually, bees have no problem travelling as far as three kilometres from their hives when foraging for nectar. But these days, after collecting nectar, bees cannot remember their way back home and get lost. Unable to reach their hives, they die. In a way, it is because of bees that we have food. Bees play a vital role in the preservation of Nature and society. They pollinate the plants that provide us with fruit and grains. Similarly, humankind benefits from each and every living creature. All beings on earth depend on one another for survival. If the engine of a plane is damaged, it cannot fly. But even if just a single vital screw is damaged, the plane also cannot fly. Similarly, even the tiniest living being plays an important role. All living creatures need our help as well in order to survive. They are also our responsibility.

With the earth's population increasing daily, it is becoming more difficult to produce enough food and grains to meet the rising demands. To address this issue, scientists are researching various artificial methods to increase the productivity of crops, such as chemical fertilizers. As such, plants that used to take six months to produce vegetables now do so in only two months. The problem is, the nutritional value of these vegetables is in fact only one-third of what it used to be. Furthermore, the lifespan of these plants has been dramatically reduced. It is easy to see that our artificial methods are backfiring.

Nature is like a duck that lays golden eggs. But if we kill the duck and try to snatch all the golden eggs at once, we will lose everything. We must stop polluting and exploiting Mother Nature. We have to protect her in order to ensure our survival as well as the survival of future generations. Nature is the wish-fulfilling tree that gives humanity all abundance. But today, our situation is like that of a fool sawing off the very branch upon which he is sitting.

If our white-blood-cell count increases, it could be a sign of cancer. Although white blood cells are not inherently dangerous, if they increase beyond a certain point, we may fall sick. Likewise, we need Nature's resources in order to live. But if we exploit them and harm Nature, it becomes dangerous for both ourselves and for others.

Amma has a request. Each and every person on this planet should play their part in restoring harmony to Nature. First of all, we should do whatever we can to stop pollution. Factories and industries are necessary, but we need to find new ways to decrease the air and water pollution caused by them. It is also essential to build the factories far from residential areas.

In cities, the increase in the number of vehicles is one of the main causes of pollution. Already most families own at least one car. If five people who live and work near one another make a car-pool schedule and take turns driving each other to work, five cars can be replaced by one.

If an entire country were to do this, then every 100,000 cars would decrease to 20,000. Pollution would be radically reduced and so much oil would be saved. We all know oil is rapidly diminishing. By car-pooling like this, our oil will last longer, but most importantly, love and cooperation will increase amongst people. Amma feels this advice is something we can all try to put into action.

When we travel short distances, instead of wasting fuel we could ride bicycles, which would also give us exercise. One of the main reasons for the increase of diseases today is lack of exercise. Some mothers complain to Amma that they spend so much money on their child's gym membership. When Amma asks them how their children get to the gym, they say they drop them off in the car, even when the gym is only a few kilometres away. If the child were to walk there, it would be enough exercise and the money for the membership could be saved.

The practice of maintaining a vegetable garden is declining. Even if we only have a tiny plot of land, we should try to grow a few vegetables, using organic fertilizers. Spending some time with our plants, we should talk to them and kiss them. This relationship with Nature will give us a new vitality.

Forests play the most important role in maintaining Nature's harmony. It is only due to them that there is any semblance of harmony in the world today. Each country should try to protect its remaining forests and plant as many trees as possible. Individually, we should each make a vow to plant at least one tree a month so that in a year, each person will plant 12 trees. If everyone participates, in just a short period we can restore Nature's beauty to the face of the world. Amma has heard of a particular type of tree [the Tabonuco Tree of the Caribbean], whose roots intertwine and graft with those of its fellow trees. Regardless of how strong the wind, the trees are not uprooted. When we live harmoniously with Nature in love and unity, we will have the strength to overcome any crisis.

Nature is our first mother. She nurtures us throughout our lives. Our birth mother may allow us to sit on her lap for a couple of years, but Mother Nature patiently bears our weight our entire life. She sings us to sleep, feeds us and caresses us. Just as a child is obligated to his birth mother, we should all feel an obligation and responsibility towards Mother Nature. If we forget this responsibility, it is equal to forgetting our own self. If we forget Nature, we will cease to exist, for to do so is to walk towards death.

In the old days, there was no specific need for environmental preservation because protecting Nature was part of worshiping God and life itself. More than remembering "God," the people used to love and serve Nature and society. They saw the Creator through the creation. They loved, worshiped and protected Nature as the visible form of God.

Let us try to reawaken this attitude. At present, the biggest threat to mankind is not a third world war, but the loss of Nature's harmony and our widening separation from Nature. We should develop the awareness of a person at gunpoint. Only then can humanity survive.

Life becomes fulfilled when humankind and Nature move together, hand in hand, in harmony. When melody and rhythm complement each other, the music becomes beautiful and pleasing to the ear. Likewise, when people live in accordance with the laws of Nature, life becomes like a beautiful song.

Nature is a huge flower garden. The animals, birds, trees, plants and people are the garden's fully blossomed flowers of diverse colours. The beauty of this garden is complete only when all of these exist as a unity, thereby spreading the vibrations of love and oneness. May all our minds become one in love. Let us work together to prevent these diverse flowers from withering away, so that the garden may remain eternally beautiful.

Amma would now like to share a few more points she feels are worth reflecting on.

1. Imagine the human race was removed from the face of the earth. The planet would once again become lush with vegetation. The water and the air would become pure. All of Nature would be filled with joy. Conversely, imagine that there was no life on earth except for human beings. We would be unable to survive. This earth created by God and the song arising from Nature are in

perfect tune and rhythm. It is only human beings who bring in notes of dissonance.

2. The source of peace and harmony is love and compassion. Through love, the tender bud of our hearts will blossom. Then the beautiful fragrance of love will spread all around.

3. The bird of society has two wings: science and spirituality. These two must go hand and hand, as both are needed for the progress of society. If we hold on to spiritual values while moving forward, then science can become a tool to bring about world peace and harmony.

4. We must never lose our inner strength. Only weak minds see the dark side of everything and become confused. Those with optimism see the rays of God's grace in any kind of darkness. The lamp of this faith is within us. Light this lamp; it will shower light to guide each and every step we take. Let us not remain stuck in the painful memories of the wars and conflicts of days past. Forget the dark history of hatred and rivalry and welcome a new era of faith, love and unity. For this, we must all work together. No effort, no matter how small, will ever be wasted. Even if

just one flower blossoms in the middle of a desert, at least it's something. This is the attitude to develop when performing actions. Our abilities may be limited, but if we row the boat of life with the paddle of self-effort, then the wind of God's grace will definitely come to assist us.

5. We should be ready to change. Otherwise, we will be forced to change. If not change, then death—we have to choose one or the other.

6. The human race should understand that it's not the only species with a right to life. How many species have already become extinct! It's not enough to have kindness and compassion for human beings; we need to have such compassion towards all living beings.

7. We will not be able to escape from disease just by destroying populations of mosquitoes, chickens and cows. The restoration of Nature's harmony should be our first priority.

If the source of war is in the mind of man, then the source of peace resides there also. If we want to prevent war in the future, we need to start inculcating values in our children at a young age. If we want to make yogurt, all we need to do is add a small amount of yogurt to some milk, stir it and allow it to sit for some time. Similarly, when parents set a good example, they impart positive values to their children. Then noble qualities spontaneously arise within the children.

When Amma travels around the globe, people from war-stricken countries often come to see her. Women from these areas tell Amma, "We wake up in the morning to the sounds of gun-fire and screaming. Our children cling to us in fear and cry; we also hold onto them and cry. It's been so many years since we awoke to the chirping of birds." Let us pray that the crackle of gunfire in such places is soon replaced by the sweet sounds of chirping birds, and that the young and old alike burst into laughter instead of tears.

Amma often feels that it would be so beautiful if—like in some child's game—instead of shrapnel, bombs scattered chocolates and candy, or spread a beautiful fragrance, or illuminated the sky with all the colours of the rainbow. If only the flashes of destruction were flashes of compassion. With modern weapons, targets can be pinpointed with deadly accuracy. If only we could reach out compassionately to the poor, the hungry and the homeless with that same precision!

Let us stand together and show the world that compassion, love and concern for our fellow beings have not completely vanished from the face of this earth. Let us build a new world of peace and harmony by remaining deeply rooted in the universal values that have nourished humanity since time immemorial. Let us say goodbye to war and brutality forever, reducing them to the stuff of fairytales. Let us be remembered in the future as the generation of peace.

||Om lokah samastah sukhino bhavantu||

Book Catalog
By Author

Sri Mata Amritanandamayi Devi
108 Quotes On Faith
108 Quotes On Love
Compassion, The Only Way To Peace:
  Paris Speech
Cultivating Strength And Vitality
Living In Harmony
May Peace And Happiness Prevail:
  Barcelona Speech
May Your Hearts Blossom:
  Chicago Speech
Practice Spiritual Values And Save The
  World: Delhi Speech
The Awakening Of Universal
  Motherhood: Geneva Speech
The Eternal Truth
The Infinite Potential Of Women:
  Jaipur Speech
Understanding And Collaboration
  Between Religions
Unity Is Peace: Interfaith Speech

Swami Amritaswarupananda Puri
Ammachi: A Biography
Awaken Children, Volumes 1-9
From Amma's Heart
Mother Of Sweet Bliss
The Color Of Rainbow

Swami Jnanamritananda Puri
Eternal Wisdom, Volumes 1-2

Swami Paramatmananda Puri
On The Road To Freedom Volumes 1-2
Talks, Volumes 1-6

Swami Purnamritananda Puri
Unforgettable Memories

Swami Ramakrishnananda Puri
Eye Of Wisdom
Racing Along The Razor's Edge
Secret Of Inner Peace
The Blessed Life
The Timeless Path
Ultimate Success

Swamini Krishnamrita Prana
Love Is The Answer
Sacred Journey
The Fragrance Of Pure Love
Torrential Love

M.A. Center Publications
1,000 Names Commentary
Archana Book (Large)
Archana Book (Small)
Being With Amma
Bhagavad Gita
Bhajanamritam, Volumes 1-6
Embracing The World
For My Children
Immortal Light
Lead Us To Purity
Lead Us To The Light
Man And Nature
My First Darshan
Puja: The Process Of Ritualistic
  Worship
Sri Lalitha Trishati Stotram

Amma's Websites

AMRITAPURI—Amma's Home Page
Teachings, Activities, Ashram Life, eServices, Yatra, Blogs and News
http://www.amritapuri.org

AMMA (Mata Amritanandamayi)
About Amma, Meeting Amma, Global Charities, Groups and Activities and Teachings
http://www.amma.org

EMBRACING THE WORLD®
Basic Needs, Emergencies, Environment, Research and News
http://www.embracingtheworld.org

AMRITA UNIVERSITY
About, Admissions, Campuses, Academics, Research, Global and News
http://www.amrita.edu

THE AMMA SHOP—Embracing the World® Books & Gifts Shop
Blog, Books, Complete Body, Home & Gifts, Jewelry, Music and Worship
http://www.theammashop.org

IAM—Integrated Amrita Meditation Technique®
Meditation Taught Free of Charge to the Public, Students, Prisoners and Military
http://www.amma.org/groups/north-america/projects/iam-meditation-classes

AMRITA PUJA
Types and Benefits of Pujas, Brahmasthanam Temple, Astrology Readings, Ordering Pujas
http://www.amritapuja.org

GREENFRIENDS
Growing Plants, Building Sustainable Environments, Education and Community Building
http://www.amma.org/groups/north-america/projects/green-friends

FACEBOOK
This is the Official Facebook Page to Connect with Amma
https://www.facebook.com/MataAmritanandamayi

DONATION PAGE
Please Help Support Amma's Charities Here:
http://www.amma.org/donations

www.ingramcontent.com/pod-product-compliance
Lightning Source LLC
Chambersburg PA
CBHW061346040426
42444CB00011B/3105